Montreal's
BEST BYOB
Restaurants

JOANNA FOX

Montreal's

BEST

Y O

B

Restaurants

2009-2010

Véhicule Press

Véhicule Press acknowledges the support of the Government of Canada's Book Industry Development Program

Cover and title page design: David Drummond
Inside imaging: Simon Garamond
Printing: Marquis Book Printing Inc.

CATALOGUING IN PUBLICATION DATA

Fox, Joanna, 1980-
Montreal's best BYOB restaurants / Joanna Fox.
Includes index.

ISBN: 978-1-55065-249-9

1. Restaurants—Québec (Province)—Montréal—Guidebooks.
2. Montréal (Québec)—Guidebooks. I. Title.

TX907.5.C22 M6 2009   647.95714'28   C2009-900681-2

Published by Véhicule Press
P.O.B. 125, Place du Parc Station
Montréal, Québec H2X 4A3

514.844.6073   FAX 514.844.7543

www.vehiculepress.com
www.cheapthrillsguides.com

CANADIAN DISTRIBUTION
LitDistCo
www.litdistco.ca
800-591-6250

U.S. DISTRIBUTION
Independent Publishers Group, Chicago, Illinois
www.ipgbook.com
800-888-4741

Printed in Canada on 100% post-consumer recycled paper.

To the memory of my grandmother, Doris Cloran,
a lover of food and all the fine things in life.

Contents

Acknowledgements

Without the help of all these hungry, generous people, I would have been a lonely diner and this book would have not been possible. First and foremost, thank you to my parents, Bill and Pat Fox, by far subjected to the most BYOBs with constant enthusiasm, support, encouragement and wine. I would also like to thank Bill Brownstein, Simon Dardick and Véhicule Press for believing in me and giving me the chance to create this guide. To all my friends and family who ate and drank, it's finally done! Andrea Fox, Ross, Mich, Kim and Grant Cloran, Dan Haber, Jon Webb (special thanks for all the duds) Bobby Shore, Pat Kiely, Matt Silver, Darren and Jared Curtis, Rich Joyner, Alex McKinnon, Caity Taylor, Tate Snidal, Katye Stevens, Mark Slutsky, Pam Czerwinski, Ben Dernis, Isabelle Pilon, Trevor Barnes, Paul Renaud, Jen Kaminski, Ben Marsh, Brandi-Ann Milbrandt, Sarah Hoida, Andrew Pink, Alex Price, Gab Taraboulsy, Kathy Acimovic, Charles D'Angelo, Kieran Crilly, Anthony Young-Brault, Steph Gurd, Adam Gollner, Josh Brown, Mauricio Lobos, Brett Stabler, Douglas Bensadoun and family, Rebecca Wolf, Fannie Crepin, Dana Klyszejko, Nadia Niro, Jess Roszler, Derek Molloy, Fred Chabot, Murad Meshgini, Eloi Dion, John Tsavalas, Steph Hanna (for the thought), Peter and Lyda Rollit and the ever-ready BYOB diners, Mark and Judy Zimmerman.

Introduction

Montreal is one of the best food cities in North America. Not only do Montrealers love to eat out, there are an enormous variety of affordable eateries, along with our passion for all things gastronomic. A large part of this city's dining charm is the Bring-Your-Own-Bottle restaurant. There are BYOB restaurants in other places in North America, but Montreal wins hands down for quality and variety.

In the late seventies people were offered the option of dining out and bringing their own bottles of wine (with no corkage fees charged). Begun on Prince-Arthur street, still a BYOB hot spot today, it quickly spread to Duluth street where the first BYOB, Le Jardin de Panos (1978), is still thriving. Montrealers have embraced these restaurants, enjoying their own wine and a great restaurant deal. Today there are over 200 BYOBs in the Montreal area which attract people in droves, bottles in hand.

Because of the number of BYOB restaurants there is a clear need for a new and concise guide. You will probably find some familiar restaurants with solid reputations, some that are go-to places when cooking at home is a tedious task, and some new gems to enjoy and share with friends. The choices range from French, Italian, and Greek, to Thai, Japanese, Vietnamese, Indian, Afghani, African and Portuguese; it's all here, right next door.

Eating out in this city is a convivial experience, as is sharing wine. You can enjoy the quality of food that Montreal has built a reputation on, and save on wine mark-ups by bringing your favorite wine with you. This is a guide to 60 great restaurants on the island of Montreal. I hope you will appreciate these places as much as I do. So eat, drink and partake of this city's thriving BYOB scene to the fullest—here is a year's worth of wonderful weekly choices.

Alphabetical List of Restaurants

Àl'Os 15
Al Dente Trattoria 16
Alex H 17
Alexandre 18
Apollo 19
Après le Jour 20

Bitoque 21
Bleu Raisin, Le 22
Bombay Mahal 23

Camelia des Tropiques 24
Campagnola, La 25
Cash & Cari 26
Caverne Grecque, Le 27
Christophe 28
Chuch Végé Thaï Express 29
Co Ba 30
Colombe, La 31
Couscous Royal, Le 32

Delices de l'Ile Maurice, Les 33

Entrepont, L' 34
Estiatorio la Porte Grecque 35

Feuille de Menthe 36
Fornarina, La 37
Fou d'Épices, Le 38

Héritiers, Les 39

Il Trullo 40
Ilios 41
India's Oven 42
Infidèles, Les 43

À l'Os

Although the majority of BYO restaurants are fairly laid-back, no-frills places, there are a few standouts that lend themselves to a special occasion and a really good bottle of wine. Definitely on the higher end of the dining scale, À l'Os offers haute cuisine with matching service in a very chic and polished environment. With its stunning open kitchen being the main attraction of the dining room, they hit all the right notes with crisp, clean décor and front window overlooking Boulevard St-Laurent. The food is French, the produce is of the highest quality. Á l'Os has some nice touches with their water menu that includes a selection of still and sparkling waters from around the world, a five-course degustation menu for $55, with more-than-generous amuse-bouches to start.

The appetizers offer some interesting options like ostrich tartare with truffle oil, scallops with cream of watercress and espelette peppers, and an absolutely mouthwatering gâteau de boudin noir—blood sausage that will make even the most wary diner go for a second bite. The mains include a Black Angus filet mignon served with a generous portion of marrow, a perfectly-seared pepper-encrusted tuna steak with carmelized endives, and a variety of game and daily specials. For dessert, try the house-made ice cream in a variety of original flavours. À l'Os is a special treat and an opportunity to dress up and truly enjoy yourself.

5207 St-Laurent (at Fairmount)
514-270-7055
Metro: Laurier, or St-Laurent, then bus 55 (north)
Hours: Tues-Sun 6-10pm
Terrace: No
Cards: Major cards
Vegetarian friendly: No
Wheelchair access: A couple of steps
Price: starters $10-$27; mains $28-$55

Al Dente Trattoria

For a good Italian meal in a friendly neighbourhood resto, look no further than Al Dente in NDG. Always a favourite with Monkland Village regulars, this BYO is great for satisfying a pasta or pizza craving in a relaxed environment. The semi-basement venue is warm and cozy in the winter, and the street-front terrace is a popular spot for a light summer meal. The wood-burning oven guarantees delicious pizzas with almost 30 combinations to choose from. The crust is light, crisp and thin, and the toppings are interesting and varied, making pizzas one of the most popular items on the menu. Another one of Al Dente's specialties is their fresh, homemade pasta, which you get to mix and match with a variety of sauces. There's a table d'hôte menu every night with additional pastas, pizzas, meat and fish, served with the soup of the day or a salad. Al Dente also offers catering, pick-up, and delivery. Open since 1989, this is a real family-style restaurant. Reservations are recommended; it's surprising how fast the place fills up.

5768 Monkland Ave., NDG (at Melrose)
514-486-4343
Metro: Villa Maria, then bus 103
Hours: Mon-Thurs 11:30am-10pm; Fri 11:30am-11pm; Sat 12-11pm; Sun 12-10pm
Cards: Major cards, Interac
Terrace: Yes
Vegetarian friendly: Yes
Wheelchair access: No
Price: starters $4.45-$9.25; mains $11.50-$14.95

Alex H

This NDG BYO is the place to go for a simple, home-cooked meal. A great staple for those who live in the neighbourhood, Alex H offers a table d'hôte menu. The restaurant itself feels more like a storefront, with tiled floors, bright track lighting and a scattering of tables and chairs. Although not the most romantic spot on the block, the food itself is impressive, as is the service. The table d'hôte includes the soup of the day or a salad, and the mains come with either pasta or potatoes, and perfectly-cooked, crunchy seasonal vegetables. The rack of lamb is lean, tender and nicely seasoned. The tasty Madagascar scallops are served in a cream sauce with mushrooms and garlic over pasta. The liver is another choice that will definitely leave you satisfied. There is a selection of house-made desserts. The apple crumble with vanilla ice cream, as well as their chocolate mousse are pure comfort food and well worth the price. Alex H has long been an NDG standard and if it isn't in your neighbourhood, it's worth the trip.

5862 Sherbrooke W. (at Clifton)
514-487-5444
Metro: Vendome, then bus 105
Hours: Wed-Fri 12-2pm; Tues-Sun 5:30-9pm, Fri-Sat 5:30-10pm
Cards: Major cards, Interac
Terrace: Yes
Vegetarian friendly: Yes, limited
Wheelchair access: Yes
Price: mains $14.50-$24.50

Alexandre

This brochetterie is no frills Greek food at reasonable prices. Boasting panoramic views (of what exactly, I could not tell), this two storey, two-terraced restaurant is a massive Greek food-producing operation. The wall-to-wall carpeting, standard tables and chairs, solarium façade, and lots of plants reminds me of places my grandparents would take me when I was young. The waiters are older, curt-and to-the-point gentlemen who don't minimally engage in conversation. The appetizers are pretty standard, but the mains are reason enough to give this place the green light. Appetizers aren't required here; the portions are generous and the price includes soup and salad, followed by your choice of main dish with rice, potatoes and a medley of steamed veggies. The chicken is plump and juicy, seasoned with a perfect blend of herbs and spices; the steaks are generous and cooked to order; and the potatoes are crispy. This is not a place where the service or decor will sweep you off your feet, but if you want a satisfying meal of typical Greek fare, check out Alexandre.

518 Duluth E. (at Berri)
514-849-4251
Metro: Mont-Royal or Sherbrooke
Hours: Mon-Sun 11am-11pm
Cards: Major cards, Interac
Terrace: Yes
Vegetarian friendly: Yes
Wheelchair access: Yes
Price: starters $2.50-$10.95; mains $10.95-$20.95

Apollo

The concept behind Chef Giovanni Apollo's newest venture is both modern and ambitious. The menu, listed on the blackboard, is always changing according to season and availability, and goes something like this: orzo, bio baby peas, foie gras, lobster, seafood, scallops, duck, caribou, deer, and pheasant. The idea behind the simplicity of this menu is that you order the dishes and they come three or four ways, all of which the diner has left in the creative hands of the kitchen. (And what a gorgeous kitchen it is, where you can see all the action while you eat.) For example, baby peas were presented on a square wooden tray in separate geometrically shaped white ceramic dishes; then there was a delicious pea risotto, peas with mushrooms and butter, a cold pea purée in a tall shot glass, and a pea flan with the consistency of a mousse. The duck was served magret, smoked and confit while the seafood was two different kinds of fish with different vegetable purées and a cold shellfish salad with apples. The desserts follow suit with a selection of cheese, fruits, chocolates, crème brulées, ice creams and sorbets, or the chef's inspiration—a varied selection. Although a few of the dishes just fell short, Apollo's ideas are fun, different and a nice change for a BYO restaurant.

6389 St-Laurent Blvd. (at Beaubien)
514-274-0153
www.apolloglobe.com
Metro: Beaubien, then bus 18 (west)
Hours: Tues-Sat 5:30-10:00pm
Cards: Major cards, Interac
Terrace: No
Vegetarian friendly: Yes
Wheelchair access: Yes, entrance steps
Price: $62 (avg.)

Après le Jour

If you're looking for a slightly sexier place to BYO, this might be your next dining destination of choice. With its subdued red lighting, table lamps, plush banquettes and burlesque décor, Après le Jour is very popular with the thirty-something crowds. On weekends the restaurant has a special table d'hôte that includes soup of the day, appetizer, main, dessert and coffee for $34. During the week order the table d'hôte at $28 and get the second meal for only $14. The service is friendly and the waiters, who rush around the two separate dining areas, are incredibly efficient. The excellent food leans towards the French classics. There are beef and salmon tartares to start with, a pleasant rillette of duck, ris-de-veau and chèvre melt with honey on savory bread. So that the next course can be enjoyed with a fresh perspective there is a choice of spiked palate cleansers, including the Long Island iced tea with lemon sorbet and Le Bikini, a coconut sorbet with dark rum. For mains, the veal saltimbocca is appropriately medium-rare, as are the lamb and the bison medallions. The rather unexpected Tandoori chicken with saffron risotto is inspired—the chicken having been marinated in a yogurt sauce for 24 hours. There is a wide selection of desserts, the café au lait panna cotta being particularly noteworthy. This popular eatery serves up substantial French cuisine in an appealing atmosphere.

901 Rachel E. (at St-André)
514-527-4141
www.restoapreslejour.com
Metro: Mont-Royal
Hours: Tues-Sun 5-10pm
Cards: Major cards, Interac
Terrace: No
Vegetarian friendly: Limited
Wheelchair access: Call ahead
Price: starters $9-$22; mains $24-$34

Bitoque

The gentrification of the Atwater/St-Henri area has finally resulted in a BYO, and a Portuguese one to boot. The plethora of Portuguese restaurants in Montreal always offer toothsome food at great prices, and Bitoque is no exception. With a BYO license since January 2009, the restaurant is spacious and stylish, with hardwood floors, a banquette lining one wall and an open kitchen. The downstairs area accommodates 50-60 people for parties and special functions. The menu has tapas-style dishes that can serve as appetizers or can be shared, notably, the lightly-fried cod balls served with a citrus chutney, grilled calamari with a drizzle of sweet paprika oil and fresh lemon, and the chorizo served on a small vegetable frittata. For mains there is great choice of seafood, chicken, lamb and beef. The Portuguese bouillabaisse is highly recommended: chock-full with clams, monkfish, shrimp, scallops and cod in a tomato saffron broth, the soup is a standout and well worth $27. The braised fall-off-the-bone lamb shank was served with roasted potatoes and vegetables. Try the restaurant's namesake, the Bitoque da casa, an AAA strip loin steak with a poached egg, meat glaze and crispy, finely-cut fries. There is also a table d'hôte that changes regularly. The Bitoque experience is one you will want to repeat.

3706 Notre-Dame W (at Bourget)
514-303-6402
Metro: Lionel Groulx, then bus 191
Hours: Mon-Thurs 5-10pm; Fri-Sat 5-11; Sun: functions only
Cards: Major cards, Interac
Terrace: No
Vegetarian Friendly: Yes
Wheelchair access: Yes, a couple entrance steps
Price: starters $5-$10; mains $18-28

Bleu Raisin, Le

This charming French restaurant is an impeccable choice for an authentic meal out. Emphasizing the freshest Quebec produce, Le Bleu Raisin offers up-market cuisine in a lovely bistro environment. The lighting is dim, the décor is subtle and the service is what you would expect from a quality French restaur-ant. The menu, chalkboard style, changes according to seasonal availability. There are usually five starters and five mains to choose from with an emphasis on meat. Le Raisin Bleu takes advantage of Quebec's wonderful local specialties such as caribou, deer, ostrich, lamb and duck. The starters range from foie gras and escargots to ostrich tartare, and for main courses, succulent duck breast, fall-off-the-bone lamb shank and always a fish of the day. The desserts include the usual French special-ties, as well as a Quebec cheese plate served with crispy baguette. Thanks to lovely restaurants like Bleu Raisin, diners get to sample some of the best of what Quebec has to offer. Reservations recommended.

5237 St-Denis (at Boucher)
514-271-2333
www.lebleuraisin.com
Metro: Laurier
Hours: Tues-Sat 5:30-10:30pm
Cards: Visa, Interac
Terrace: Yes
Vegetarian friendly: No
Wheelchair access: Yes
Price: starters $12-$24; mains $29-$34

Bombay Mahal

In the heart of Montreal's Little India is one of the city's best hole-in-the-wall Indian restaurants. Although not much to look at, the constantly busy Bombay Mahal offers excellent, wholesome, ridiculously cheap Indian fare with a spicy kick for those who like to ride the endorphin chili high. Some highlights of the menu are the channa samosas, stuffed with potatoes, peas and spices and served drenched in a chickpea (channa), tomato, coriander and yoghurt sauce. The vegetable pakoras come with a phenomenal green chili, mint and yoghurt sauce. All the vegetable dishes have great flavour and complexity. The tardka dhal, a yellow lentil dish, and the eggplant bharta, are both creamy, rich and spicy. The vindaloo is definitely hot, but the flavours of cardamom and cinnamon entice the palate before the jolt of chili hits you (and it will). The tandoori chicken is a bit disappointing (memories of childhood 'shake and bake' come to mind) but the chicken tikka is a nice break from the other spices with a milder seasoned flavour. The Indian breads are always a favorable way to overindulge so try the delicious chicken naan or the aloo paratha, stuffed with potatoes and spices. This is a phenomenal deal for a truly terrific meal.

1001 Jean-Talon W. (at Birnam)
514-273-3331
Metro: L'Acadie
Hours: Tues-Sat 11am-10pm; Sun 11am-9pm
Cards: Interac
Terrace: No
Vegetarian friendly: Yes
Wheelchair access: No
Price: starters $3-6, mains $8-$11

Camelia des Tropiques

This sunny, happily-decorated place is a comfortable and amicable dining environment. At Camelia des Tropiques, the table d'hôte is a steal including their signature aromatic Tonkonese soup (with a choice of vegetable, chicken or beef), a fried spring roll or rice paper roll, main dish and dessert for about $22. There are plenty of other choices on the menu including simple grilled chicken on a bed of greens with a lightly-sweetened rice vinegar dressing (Goi ga) being particularly tasty. The flavours here are refined and delicate with an adept use of fresh herbs and spices. The Camelia signature duck dish is lovely, with pieces of the indulgent crispy skin scattered on top. The spicy sizzling shrimp is not as spicy as its two-chili ranking on the menu, but they will happily offer freshly minced chilies to perk up any dish. There is also a lighter menu for those who want to watch their waistlines. The service is mildly attentive at best, so don't be surprised if you rarely have your server checking on your table.

5024 Cote-des-Neiges (at Queen Mary)
514-738-8083
Metro: Cote-des-Neiges, or Guy-Concordia, then bus 165
Hours: Tues-Fri 11:30am-2pm; 5:30-9:30pm;
    Sat-Sun 5:30-9:30pm
Cards: Major cards, Interac
Terrace: No
Vegetarian friendly: Yes
Wheelchair access: Yes
Price: starters $3.50-$7; mains $10-$15

Campagnola, La

Run by two convivial brothers, Joe and Dino Arcoraci, this LaSalle BYO is a lovely choice for a fabulous Italian meal out. La Campagnola has recently undergone a bit of a revamp, with a more elaborate menu and an improvement to the deli-style décor in the main dining room. With their friendly, considerate staff clad in referee-striped Pirelli shirts, there is no mistaking the Italian roots here. The deli counter, open all day, offers sauces, cheeses, and house specialties. Dinner selections range from oven-baked rabbit and grilled veal braccioli to exceptional osso bucco. On Wednesdays they offer a leg of lamb dinner ($29) which they carve at the table. For groups of six or more, call 24 hours in advance. Everything the brothers serve is superb, and choosing from their most popular dishes, marked with a star on the menu, is recommended. The tomato, feta, olive and basil salad is very appetizing, with fresh tomatoes harvested from the family garden in summer. The chicken or veal with cream, cognac and roasted red bell peppers will have you licking your plate. A catering service is also available for parties and business fuctions. The Campagnola crew have covered all the bases—creating a real family recipe for success.

1714 Dollard Ave., Lasalle (at Rejane)
514-363-4066
www.lacampagnola.ca
Metro: Angrignon, then bus 106
Hours: Tues-Thurs and Sun 4:30-10pm; Fri-Sat 4:30-11pm;
    closed Mon
Cards: Major cards, Interac
Terrace: Yes
Vegetarian friendly: Yes
Wheelchair access: Yes
Price: starters $8-$19; mains $17-$36

Cash & Cari

Plateau residents can rejoice again. Nantha is back. After a couple of years hiatus, Nantha Kumar has reopened with Cash & Cari. Gracing us with deliciously affordable Malaysian, Indonesian and Thai creations, Nantha's signature spices (and Plateau celebrity status) are still very much intact. The new place is part restaurant, part gallery with artists' work adorning the walls of this intimate and relaxed dining space. The changing menu, written on various chalkboards scattered around the room, is small and simple with daily specials and take-out available. Sarters include samosas and a soup of the day, with the main courses offering phad Thai and a selection curries with various meat, chicken and seafood combinations. The spicy phad Thai is a great heaping serving. The Thai green curry is superb with tender pieces of chicken and potatoes nestled in the savory sauce. Excellent Malaysian lamb curry is also a Nantha specialty. For those who mourned Nantha's Kitchen, lovers of spice and the next generation of devotees, Cash & Cari is a wonderful place of rebirth.

68 Duluth E. (at Coloniale)
514-284-5696
Metro: Mont-Royal
Hours: Tues-Sat: 6-10pm
Cards: Cash only
Terrace: A few tables on the street
Vegetarian friendly: No
Wheelchair access: Yes
Price: starters $3-$8; mains $12-$17

Caverne Grecque, Le

It's often hard to discern one restaurant from the next on Prince Arthur. After careful sampling, lots of lively debate and eventually process of elimination, Le Caverne Grecque has come out on top. The inside of this Greek dining locale is cozier and more inviting than many along this pedestrian mall. With brick walls, wood paneling, lots of real plants, both planted along the walls and hanging from the ceiling, skylights, soft yellow lighting, candles and spacious dark wood tables, you're comfortably at home, as soon as you sit down. The staff is both accommodating and efficient and the food is pleasant, hearty Greek fare. With two storeys, there is plenty of room for groups and parties, but still manages to maintain a sense of intimacy. Most meals come with choice of soup or salad, and the portions are more than worth the price. The sirloin is an example of a dish that goes above and beyond expectations—juicy, cooked to order and delicious. The butterfly shrimp with their signature garlic sauce is a treat, and the chicken brochette is always a safe bet. So if you happen to be strolling along Prince Arthur and are looking for your best shot at a Greek meal, Caverne Grecque will not disappoint.

105 Prince Arthur E. (at Coloniale)
514-844-5114
Metro: Sherbrooke, or St-Laurent, then bus 55 north
Hours: Mon-Sun 11am-11pm
Cards: Major cards
Terrace: Yes
Vegetarian friendly: Yes
Wheelchair access: No
Price: starters: $4.25-$11.95; mains $12.95-$28.95

Christophe

There is a small group of restaurants under the BYO umbrella that really don't feel like the typical bring-your-own-wine places. The décor is more polished, the plating beautifully executed, and the service more attentive. Christophe is a French restaurant in Outremont that defines French Bistro to a T. From the male servers smartly dressed in white shirts and ties, to the checkered tile floors, the wood bar, mirrored wall, bistro tables and classic French dishes, this is an irresistible neighbourhood spot. Chef Christophe Geffray's menu offers table d'hôte or degustation options. All main courses include either soup (reflecting the season) or appetizer of the day. You can choose appetizers such as seafood ravioli and the decadent foie gras crème brulée with wild mushrooms. The mains can include roast loin of veal with orange zest or a surf-and-turf combo of quail and scallops, usually accompanied by miniature root vegetables. Dessert is an option, but a well-selected Quebec cheese plate is a perfect to end this fabulous food. Reservations essential.

1187 Van Horne (at De L'Épée)
514-270-0850
www.restaurantchristophe.com
Metro: Outremont, or Place-des-Arts, then bus 80
Hours: Tues-Sat: 6-10pm
Cards: Visa, MC, Interac
Terrace: No
Vegetarian friendly: No
Wheelchair access: Yes
Price: starters $7.50-$16; mains $34-$38

Chuch Végé Thaï Express

Chu Chai is well known as one of Montreal's best, slightly upscale vegetarian eateries. Directly next door is Chuch Végé Thaï Express, a more relaxed, less expensive counterpart with a take-out counter and dining room. The food is just as good, the service casual, and the atmosphere almost Zen-like. With its brick walls, dark wood paneling and concrete floors, Chuch is equally appropriate for a refreshing lunch as it is for an intimate dinner. The chef, Lily Sirikittikul, truly an innovator in her field, is serving up delicious Thai food in an all-vegetarian menu. What makes this food so unique is the kitchen's re-creation of fish, duck, beef, chicken and prawns so that they are vegetarian, but taste eerily like the real thing. The duck (my personal favourite) truly has the flavour and texture of duck, the prawns really look like prawns, and it is hard to belief that the beef and broccoli is meat-free. Sirikittikul's dishes are vibrant and full of fresh herbs, spices and great produce. There is also a selection of tofu and strictly vegetable options. This woman knows her food and has filled a vegetarian niche that has even carnivores impressed. For the summer, there is also a terrace out front, which makes this place a not-to-be-missed vegetarian dining destination.

4088-4094 St-Denis (at Duluth)
514-843-4194
www.chuchai.com
Metro: Mont-Royal or Sherbrooke
Hours: 11:30am-10pm daily
Cards: Visa, Interac
Terrace: Yes
Vegetarian friendly: Yes
Wheelchair access: Four entrance steps
Prices: mains $10-$12

Co Ba

Co Ba isn't quite Japanese, Szechwan or Thai cuisine. It's a mélange of all three, wrapped up into a simple menu of predominantly chicken and seafood dishes with a varied selection of sushi. This is a fine place to satisfy your pan-Asian cravings when you can't quite decide which direction to take. The décor is subtle and the tables are well spaced with comfortable highback chairs. There is plenty of room for groups and the staff is friendly and helpful. For starters there are soups, spicy calamari salad and Hunan dumplings in peanut sauce that are plump and tasty. The main courses range from standards like General Tao chicken, phad Thai and teriyaki dishes, to your choice of chicken, shrimp or a generous seafood combo of shrimp, scallops and salmon served with a variety of sauces (Thai basil and lemongrass, yellow curry, ginger). The yellow curry is surprisingly drier and spicier than the usual Thai curries, but a pleasant change; the Thai basil sauce is aromatic and sweet. The sushi is reasonable and offers enough choice for any aficionado, keeping in mind this isn't specifically a sushi restaurant. The gracious owners of Co Ba provide an upscale environment to enjoy a variety of dishes and cuisines with the BYO option.

1124 Laurier W. (at Querbes)
514-908-1889
Metro: Laurier, then bus 51, or Place-des-Arts, then bus 80
Hours: Tues-Fri: 11:30am-2:30pm, 5:30-10pm; Sat-Sun: 5:30-
  10:30pm
Cards: Major cards, Interac
Terrace: No
Vegetarian friendly: Yes
Wheelchair access: A couple steps
Price: starters $3.75-$10.95; mains $16.95-$25.95

Colombe, La

On the edge of the Duluth street dining hub, La Colombe is an elegant, yet intimate restaurant right on the corner of St-Hubert. With it's starched linen tablecloths, refined tableware and exceptional Quebec produce, La Colombe is a cut above the rest. The menu is a table d'hôte format, but there are additional appetizers to choose from, including a delicious house smoked salmon and their signature foie gras. The main courses are beautifully prepared with a selection ranging from bison filet (fabulous), to milk-fed and grain-fed veal, duck magret with sour cherry sauce, tarragon halibut with tomato and dill, leg of lamb and mignon of pork with honey and spices. It's a French food-lover's heaven with quality locally-sourced meats. The menu changes seasonally, according to freshness and availability so although they do have some staples, there is constant re-invention. Whether it's a special occasion or just the desire for an excellent meal out, La Colombe definitely deserves a good bottle of wine.

554 Duluth E. (at St-Hubert)
514-849-8844
Metro: Sherbrooke
Hours: Tues-Sat 5:30-10pm
Cards: Amex, MC, Visa
Terrace: No
Wheelchair access: Two steps
Price: Table d'hôte $42 and $55, plus extras

Couscous Royal, Le

For great Moroccan food in an eclectic atmosphere, this friendly and intimate BYO run by Anissa and Hafid Zniber is a must. The ceilings are draped with fabric to resemble a Moroccan tent and the walls are covered in colorful tapestries. If you're a group of 4 to 6, ask for the lounge-style table upstairs surrounded by a U-shaped banquette with pillows. There are two menus—the table d'hôte which includes their tasty hummus (lightly infused with lemon, garlic and olive oil and served with warm pita), an appetizer, main, dessert and aromatic tea, or an appetizer and a main course for a single price. To start, there are two pastillas—Morocco's national dish—filo pastry appetizers made with chicken, almonds, onions, cinnamon and saffron, or with a mixture of seafood. Other starters include a tomato based soup with coriander, chickpeas and lentils, a refreshing Moroccan salad of diced tomatoes, cucumbers, green peppers, onions and fresh herbs, or their house-made merguez sausages. For mains there are a variety of classic couscous dishes (vegetable, chicken, lamb, merguez), a Mechoui of roasted lamb with garlic, saffron and vegetable couscous, and a selection of tagines (chicken with green olives and confit lemon, or shrimp with tomato and coriander), all served with couscous. Moroccan pastries and tea are a sublime ending to a perfect meal.

919 Duluth E. (at St-Andre)
514-528-1307
www.lecouscousroyal.com
Metro: Sherbrooke
Hours: Thurs-Sun: 5-10pm
Cards: Major cards, Interac
Terrace: No
Vegetarian Friendly: Yes
Wheelchair Accesible: No
Price: $16.95-$24.95

Delices de l'Ile Maurice, Les

As soon as you enter this rather anonymous looking Verdun restaurant that houses Les Delices de L'Ile Maurice, you know immediately that you're in for a treat. The décor is certainly eclectic and original, with mismatched linoleum-topped tables, folding card chairs, bright walls papered in Mauritian tourist propaganda and my all-time favorite restaurant touch—tropical-themed shower curtains in the windows. Mauritius is an island just east of Madagascar and combines a mixture of Asian (Chinese and Indian), Creole and European (French, Portuguese and Danish) cuisines. From this melting pot comes Les Delices' delicious meat and seafood dishes served with a selection of sauces (curry, Creole, Cajun and saffron and tomato) as well as a small variety of appetizers such as the recommended fried chicken, and a wonderful soup of the day. Sylvester, who has blessed us with this little piece of Mauritian heaven, is a one-man show. There is no menu and I highly suggest going with an open mind and asking him what he recommends for the night. Not only is the food great, the atmosphere is like sitting in Sylvester's home kitchen (which you pretty much are) with him serving you, cooking and watching soccer matches on television in-between. This experience is truly priceless, from the crispy fried cabbage given to you when you sit down, to the sugar-covered jujubes you get for dessert. Ah, the laid back, easy, breezy island life!

272 Hickson, Verdun (at Wellington)
514-768-6023
Metro: De L'Eglise
Hours: Tues-Sat 5-10pm
Cards: Cash only
Vegetarian friendly: Doubtful
Terrace: No
Wheelchair access: Yes
Price: Inexpensive

Entrepont, L'

Yet another Montreal BYO favorite, L'Entrepont is nestled within the Plateau's residential neighbourhood. Having undergone a refreshing makeover, this tasteful, close-quartered, culinary gem is a sure bet. From the café au lait-coloured walls, efficient waiters and small bistro tables, this place screams French food. This is exactly how you want to sample this city's best, with good food, good service and a solid reputation. All meals are offered either table d'hôte or degustation—the former including soup and main course; the latter including soup, starter, trou normand, main, dessert and coffee. The soup to start changes daily and there are additional appetizer and main specials. The starters range from a rich house terrine to smoked trout, a refreshing chèvre, and a house specialty—the duo foie gras. The mains include Brome Lake duck, foie gras-stuffed quail, Cajun-styled tuna, rack of lamb and red deer with gooseberries and cracked pepper. The food is cooked with attention and care and presented with pride. The cheesecake, touted as the best in the city, is rich, sinful and heavenly. L'Entrepont has taken pains to keep up with the times—improving on their culinary style, as well as their overall presentation. This is a must for those who love French cuisine. Good wine is a must, as are reservations.

4622 Hotel-de-Ville (at Villeneuve)
514-845-1369
www.bistrolentrepont.com
Metro: Mont-Royal, or St-Laurent, then bus 55 (north)
Hours: Mon-Sat 5:30-10pm; Sun - will open for groups
Cards: MC
Terrace: No
Vegetarian friendly: No
Wheelchair access: A couple of steps
Price: starters $9; mains $28-$38

Estiatorio la Porte Grecque

Situated in a historic stone house in Dollard-des-Ormeaux (built in 1856) is a family-run Greek restaurant that offers terrific food at fabulous prices. As for the restaurant, it's been around for over 25 years and has established a solid following among West Island diners and Greek food aficionados alike. The thick stone walls add to the warm ambiance of the dining rooms. In summer, the lovely tree-shaded patio is not to be missed. The menu covers all your Greek specialties with plenty of variety in terms of meat, seafood, combos and even a page of health conscious dishes. The service is fast and friendly and the portions are more than liberal. The starter platters of hot and cold pikilia for two are enough for four people to share and are an excellent way to sample a variety of appetizers. All main courses, such as grilled spring lamb chops, swordfish brochettes, butterfly shrimps, moussaka and grilled chicken oregano are served with a salad, potatoes and rice, and they hit all the right notes. For a nice meal in a beautiful setting, you will surely leave La Porte Grecque satisfied.

4600 Sources Blvd., DDO (at 9th)
514-683-4482
www.laportegrecque.com
Hours: Mon-Fri 10:45am-10pm; Sat-Sun 5-10pm
Cards: Major cards, Interac
Terrace: Yes
Vegetarian friendly: Yes
Wheelchair access: Yes
Price: starters $2.25-$10.95; mains $5.95-$20.95

Feuille de Menthe

This Vietnamese restaurant, run by a hospitable mother and daughter team, is a real find. The decor is sophisticated and stylish with cream-coloured walls and plush red carpeting. The ceilings are high and there are lots of plants. The menu offers Vietnamese and other Asian choices including Tonkinese soup, mango and papaya salads and a variety of rice paper rolls. The rolls, made to order, are filled generously with vermicelli and fresh herbs, with an assortment of vegetable, chicken and shrimp or beef. The beef—tender strips of marinated beef served with a fish-chili dipping sauce, is highly recommended. Another excellent starter is the fried Agedashi tofu served with a delicate dressing. The mains all come with generous portions of rice or noodles. You can't go wrong with stellar dishes such as creamy seafood, mushrooms and broccoli baked in a half-coconut; sautéed beef with lemongrass; grilled basa (a type of catfish) with dill, soft shell crab; and ginger chicken with vegetables and rice. If you want something more zest, try the spicy coconut milk and curry dish. The service at Feuille de Menthe is charming, and you are sure to have a most pleasurable meal.

5136 Parc (at Laurier)
514-272-1477
Metro: Place-des-Arts, then bus 80
Hours: Tues-Fri 11am-3pm, 5-10pm; Sat-Sun 5-10pm
Cards: Visa, MC, Interac
Terrace: No
Vegetarian friendly: Yes
Wheelchair access: No
Price: starters $4-$7; mains $18-$23

Fornarina, La

La Fornarina is an old-style pasta/pizza emporium. Its mosaic-like mural of a Mediterranean setting doesn't really transport you to a cliffside terrace off the Amalfi coast, but the food and the service take you half-way there. There are no pretensions in this family-run resto—the food is delicious and inexpensive and the service is enthusiastic and friendly. The menu has a wide selection of dishes, but the pastas and brick oven pizzas are what make this BYO a mainstay. The pizzas have thin, crispy crusts, ample cheese and substantial toppings. The pastas are al dente, available in half-portions for those who just want a taste, and the lasagna is creamy and delicious. Veal is is served with your choice of pasta side, a nice alternative if you can't make up your mind. The salads hover at the $9.50 mark and are designed for sharing—one salad is good for four people. The tiramisu is made in-house. La Fornarina is relaxed, casual and just right for a little taste of Italy that's close to home.

6825 St-Laurent (at Dante)
514-271-1741
Metro: de Castelnau
Hours: Sun-Thurs 11am-10pm; Fri-Sat 11am-12am
Cards: MC, Visa
Vegetarian friendly: Yes
Wheelchair access: No
Terrace: No
Price: starters $4.95-$9.95; mains $10.95-$21.95

Fou d'Épices, Le

This lovely Vietnamese restaurant is a fine place for an inexpensive meal. It's a step up in the décor department—tasteful touches make this setting modern and comfortable. The lighting is soft and low, the service is cordial and the restaurant is usually packed. The soups are impressive. The seafood soup is outstanding with a generous overflow of scallops, prawns and crab. Pass on the imperial rolls and order the spring rolls. They're freshly rolled, stuffed with chicken, prawns, vermicelli, fresh coriander and served with a sweet peanut dipping sauce. For main dishes, there are vegetarian options and a wide selection of combinations that include soup, imperial rolls (substitute spring rolls) and a main dish. The grilled chicken, lightly seasoned with a slightly sweet soy glaze served with either steamed rice or vermicelli and sautéed vegetables, is a perfectly satisfying dish. You can also have it with beef or seafood, all equally as good. For dessert, you can't go wrong with fried banana and ice cream for a mere $3. Fou d'Épices is a great find and is sure to impress with satisfying food, service and good value.

300 Mont-Royal E. (at Henri-Julien)
514-288-8390
Metro: Mont-Royal
Hours: Tues-Fri 11am-3pm, 5-10pm; Sat-Sun 5:30-11pm
Cards: Cash only
Terrace: No
Vegetarian friendly: Yes
Wheelchair access: Not the men's room
Price: starters $4-$8; mains $10.95-$16.95

Héritiers, Les

Once again the Plateau provides us with a gem of a restaurant in a residential neighourhood. Les Héritiers is a welcoming place with the feel of a modest Paris bistro that offers delicious food with quintessential Montreal charm. The staff is extremely efficient and the food is traditional, but varied. As with many French BYOs in this city, the menu has two table d'hôte options, and a wide choice of à la carte selections. For starters there is the light and simple gravlax on fennel and salicorn, warm goat cheese salad, or more complex offerings like the terrine, duck confit or escargots with mushrooms and brie. From an alluring list of main courses, you could try guinea fowl stuffed with figs and chorizo, filet mignon with blue cheese, veal chops with mushroom sauce, duck confit, fresh scallops with basil butter, and sea bass marinated in lemon and honey. For dessert there are cheeses and a short, but well-chosen selection of sinful indulgences. The chocolate mousse cake with hazelnut biscuit and praline is well worth the calories and pairs beautifully with an after-dinner espresso. Les Héritiers is a noteworthy destination for either a special occasion or a casual weekday meal out. Reservations recommended.

5091 De Lanaudière (at Laurier)
514-528-4953
www.lesheritiers.com
Metro: Laurier, then bus 27
Hours: Tues-Sun 6-10:30pm
Cards: MC
Terrace: No
Vegetarian friendly: Limited
Wheelchair access: A couple of steps
Price: starters $7-$8; mains $19-$28

Il Trullo

Located in the heart of the Plateau, Il Trullo is a small, homey place that serves pleasant, inexpensive pastas, seafood, chicken and veal. The service is informal and relaxed and the food is basic Italian. There is also a great terrace at the front overlooking St-Denis for those who love to people watch and enjoy the buzz of a nice summer night. There is a wide selection fish and seafood, especially convenient for those who just want a little taste of pasta on the side. The lemon sole is zesty and fresh and the accompanying tomato and basil pasta is simple, flavourful and light. The table d'hôte offers a changing array of dishes that includes the soup of the day or a generous green salad. The starters include the usual Italian choices but the bruschetta is an appropriate way to begin with a cool glass of Pinot Grigio. The spaghetti Bolognese is full of meaty chunks and radiates the warmth of genuine Italian home cooking. The veal is equally pleasing—tender and lightly seasoned. The desserts are all made in-house and offer Italian specials like tiramisu and panna cotta nightly. Il Trullo offers simple, satisfying, family cuisine at reasonable prices.

4135 St. Denis (at Rachel)
514-504-1619
Metro: Mont-Royal
Hours: Tues-Fri 11:30am-10pm; Sat 5-10pm; Sun 5-9:30pm
Cards: Major cards
Terrace: Yes
Vegetarian friendly: Yes
Wheelchair access: No
Price: mains $15-$30

Ilios

It's great to find a Greek BYO that doesn't remind you of all the other Greek places in Montreal——not that they're bad, just predictable. The menu is small, focussing on seafood, and the food is impressively authentic. There are two appetizers that are not to be missed. The Greek salad is served at room temperature, the tomatoes are ripe and sweet, the feta is creamy and salty, the olives are plump and the herb dressing lifts and marries all the flavours. The next must-try starter is the Ilios special——fried eggplant and zucchini slices served with tzatziki. The vegetables are sliced thinly and ever-so lightly battered and fried. The accompanying tzatziki is garlicky and zesty. The main courses offer the usual Greek chicken and lamb dishes, but the selection of seafood and fish is exceptional. The fish are served whole, the calamari is lightly fried and tender and the grilled prawns are juicy and have that delicious charcoal taste. The meals come with potatoes, rice and lima beans in a tomato sauce. For an above- average Greek meal, with the BYO advantage, Ilios is a restaurant that is not to be overlooked.

408 Gilford (at St. Denis)
514-499-0808
Metro: Laurier, then bus 30 (north)
Hours: Mon-Sun: 5-9:30pm
Cards: Major cards, Interac
Terrace: No
Vegetarian friendly: Limited to starters and salads
Wheelchair access: Yes
Parking: Free after 5pm in the lot on Rivard and Gilford
Price: starters $6-$13; mains $14-$29

India's Oven

The Indian BYO restaurants on Jean-Talon have character and kitschy charm. They're also friendly and always a great deal. India's Oven is no exception. With high-backed banquet-style chairs and the sounds of Indian shows enveloping the room from the wall-mounted televison, it almost feels like you're actually in India. Almost. The owner cordially floats around the room, greeting everyone, answering questions, taking orders, and generally making sure everyone is okay—like he is the host at his own dinner party. It immediately puts you at ease, which is a good thing because sometimes you might have to wait a bit. But it's worth it. The savoury vegetarian samosas are delectable and give Bombay Mahal a run for their money. All dishes can be prepared to the requested level of spice and heat. The tandooris and tikkas are ideal for those who don't like saucy dishes, but the butter chicken is the real favorite here. The lamb vindaloo is also a popular choice—the richness of the lamb marrying the spices beautifully. And, unexpectedly, they serve a deer curry. All mains are served with rice or naan so there is always plenty to go around. There are many vegetarian options with the black-spiced dhal being a rare treat. India's Oven isn't breaking any culinary ground, but the food, the atmosphere and the host make for a charming Indian experience.

454 Jean-Talon W. (at Durocher)
514-509-8678
Metro: Parc, or Place des Arts, then bus 80
Hours: Sun-Tues 11am-10:30pm; Thurs-Sat 11am-11pm
Cards: Major cards, Interac
Terrace: No
Vegetarian friendly: Yes
Wheelchair access: One step
Price: starters $2.99-$7.99; mains $3.49-$15.99

Infidèles, Les

Les Infidèls is one of Montreal's most cherished BYO restaurants and rightfully so. This is excellent French cuisine with attentive service. Montreal's BYO reputation was built with the help of this consistent culinary leader. The restaurant decor is minimal and tasteful, with large windows at the front that flood the place with light, creating an intimate yet open setting. An amuse-bouche kick-starts the meal with a delectable mouthful of the chef's nightly inspirations. All main courses include the soup of the day, but there is also a selection of appetizers that are not to be overlooked. With an emphasis on seasonal Quebec produce, it is hard to make a wrong choice here. The scallop dish with fruit salsa, coconut milk and mint is exceptional. The scallops, perfectly golden-seared, have that subtle, translucent texture on the inside that makes this an irresistible treat. The wild mushroom and brie tart is slightly on the rich side, but pairs with the beautiful medley of the mushrooms to complement the cheese. The choices of mains range from meats and game including caribou and horse filet mignon, a sinful duck à l'orange, and a succulent pork and cheese dish that was a personal favorite. The selection of desserts makes it hard to choose just one, but the crème brulée *du moment* is just perfection (ours was lemon thyme and was my most memorable brulée to date). This is hands down one of the best BYO restaurants in the city and an incredible treat for gastronomes and casual diners alike.

771 Rachel E. (at St-Hubert)
514-528-8555
www.lesinfideles.ca
Metro: Mont-Royal
Hours: Wed-Fri 11:30am-2pm (groups only);
    Mon-Sun 6-10:30pm
Cards: Major cards
Vegetarian friendly: Limited
Terrace: No
Wheelchair access: Yes
Price: starters $8-$15; mains $19-$36

Jardin de Panos, Le

Jardin de Panos was the first BYO restaurant on Duluth and has been a family-run business since 1979. It's not surprising then, that Panos is packed every night. And with good reason: the food is good and consistent. With its unmistakable white and blue painted brick façade, checkered tablecloths and great summer terrace, this spot has a welcoming feeling that is perfect for that night you want to go out and eat, but you're not in the mood to go *out*, out. Service is efficient and quick, but sometimes a little too quick; so let them know if you want a longer, lazy meal. These guys turn tables faster than shots of ouzo at a Greek wedding. Try the homemade pikilia platter to start—a selection of taramosalata, olives, feta, spanakopita, dolmades and veggies. The eggplant purée is particularly delectable and perfect to spread on the crusty whole wheat bread that's provided. The fried calamari is another great pick, light and tender. The generous mains include all the Greek standards, served with potatoes and their house salad with fresh dill and a fantastic vinaigrette. The chicken brochettes are juicy; the grilled scallops are plump; and the lamb is surprisingly good quality at the price. The moussaka, a house specialty, is a little dry, but passes the test. The selection of desserts is standard, but opt for the house-made baklava to end a great meal on a true Greek note.

521 Duluth E. (at Berri)
514-521-4206
www.lejardindepanos.com/
Metro: Sherbrooke
Hours: Mon-Sun 12pm-11pm
Cards: Amex, MC, Visa
Vegetarian friendly: Yes
Terrace: Yes
Wheelchair access: No
Price: starters $2.50-$10.95; mains $14.95-$21.95

Jardin des Puits, Le

Bring-your-own-wine restaurants and Greek food seem to go hand in hand. Although many are located on Prince Arthur and Duluth, Le Jardin des Puits has been a longstanding fixture for those residents in and around the Villeneuve-Hôtel- de-Ville area. It's typical Greek with blue and white checkered table-cloths, cups for wine glasses and thick slices of whole wheat bread on every table. Although the terrace on the side is in need of a little love, it fills up all summer long. All mains come with a choice of hearty vegetable or lentil soup. There are plenty of appetizers to choose from but it's the fried calamari that's a must-try—juicy, tender and exquisite with a squeeze of fresh lemon. It's a great dish to share. For mains, the chicken bro-chettes are moist and generous, smothered in their house mus-tard sauce and the lamb cutlets—a favourite—is even better. All come with a large mound of rice, salad and potatoes and will not leave you wanting for more.

180 Villeneuve East (at Hôtel-de-Ville)
514-849-0555
www.lejardindespuits.com
Metro: Laurier, or St-Laurent, then bus 55 (north)
Cards: Major cards, Interac
Hours: Tues-Sat 11:30am-10pm (kitchen closes earlier)
Terrace: Yes
Vegetarian friendly: Yes
Wheelchair access: Yes
Price: starters $3.95-$10.95; mains $13.95-$30.95

Khyber Pass

If you're feeling adventurous and are up for something a little bit different, try the Afghani cuisine offered at Khyber Pass. Split into two rooms, the restaurant has brightly-coloured walls decorated with paintings and tapestries. As with most places on Duluth Street, the summertime heat allows the front windows to slide open and there is a terrace located at the back. When you are seated, a basket of flat bread is brought to the table with three tasty dipping sauces, all mild in flavour. The house soup—a delicious mixture of red lentils and coriander—is an ideal way to begin the meal. Another fine choice is the eggplant borani, sliced, fried and served with garlic yoghurt. All of the main courses include rice and come with an incredibly refreshing salad of cucumber, onions, tomatoes, mint and coriander—a perfect palate cleanser to compliment the Afghani spices. The Kabuli palaw is a lamb shank served on a bed of tasty brown rice with raisins and sliced carrots—a great combination of flavours. The kofta chalaw is also excellent, made up of two large, moist meatballs served in a rich tomato sauce. The vegetarian combo is a spinach, cauliflower and eggplant gumbo. There is a selection of kebabs and an aromatic rosewater and pistachio pudding for dessert. This is a BYO not to be missed. (There is also a branch at 1694 Blvd. Saint-Martin W. in Laval 450- 688-5907).

506 Duluth E. (at Berri)
514-844-7131
http://66.49.138.201/english/welcome.html
Metro: Sherbrooke
Hours: Mon-Sun 5-11pm
Cards: Visa, Interac
Vegetarian friendly: Yes
Terrace: Yes
Wheelchair access: A couple entrance steps
Price: starters $4.50-$7.50; mains $15.95-$18.95

Lele da Cuca

This little Brazilian spot is a real mom and pop kind of place. Seating no more than forty, its quaint and cozy atmosphere make it perfect to sample Brazilian fare without any gastronomic pretensions. The brightly-painted walls, refreshing food and lively décor are the perfect cure for the Montreal blues. The menu is divided into Brazilian and Mexican dishes, but opt for the Brazilian choices to soak up the real experience. The Brazilian platter for two is an excellent way to start. It includes a hearts of palm salad, pickled spiced mango (Maculele), coconut shavings pickled in lemon juice, hen giblets (Sarapatel) and black beans. Although the hen giblets are rich on their own, paired with the sweet spice of the mangoes, the deliciously refreshing coconut, the hearts of palm and the beans, this dish is surprisingly well balanced and delicious. There is not a huge selection of main dishes, but for the size of this place, it feels just right. The Arroz Pernambucano is a paella-style dish, with rice, shrimp, chicken and chicken sausage in a mildly spicy tomato sauce. The Bahiana shrimps are cooked in a spicy and creamy tomato coconut sauce and served with steamed rice. And one cannot forget Brazil's national dish— the black bean and pork feijoada. All the main dishes are served with black beans and a salad. The entire meal experience is fun, enhanced by the live music which is surprisingly unobtrusive in such a small space.

70 Marie-Anne E. (at St-Dominique)
514-849-6649
www.leledacuca.com
Metro: Mont-Royal
Hours: Noon-10pm daily
Cards: Major cards, Interac
Vegetarian friendly: Yes
Terrace: No
Wheelchair access: Yes
Price: starters $3.95-$17.95; mains $15.95-$18.95

Lotus Bleu

This small corner restaurant specializes in healthy Vietnamese cuisine. It's nice to see restaurants jumping on the health bandwagon and trying to make culinary adjustments to create a more health-conscious menu. Other than a few fried blips including the imperial rolls, crispy spinach, shrimps and other fried delights, this is a relatively low cholesterol menu. The restaurant is intimate, with lovely oriental-style chairs and the hum of Vietnamese music playing in the background. Although not very big inside, there is a spacious terrace that opens up onto the street for casual outdoor summer dining. The menu includes many meal combinations at reasonable prices, as well as a selection of appetizers, soups, grilled meats, seafood, and wok dishes. Their won ton soup is lightly aromatic and full of plump, homemade dumplings. If you are looking for the health conscious options here, go no further than the grill. Their selection of brochettes served on a bed of rice with a salad are irresistible—tender and lightly marinated. Lotus Bleu has its loyal fans. Once you have tried this neighbourhood treasure, you will understand why.

350 Duluth E. (at Drolet)
514-843-6183
Metro: Mont-Royal
Hours: Mon-Thurs 11am-10pm; Fri-Sun 4-11pm
Cards: Major cards, Interac
Terrace: Yes
Vegetarian friendly: Yes
Wheelchair access: Yes
Price: starters $1.95-$7.95; mains $9.95-$21.95

Lychee

Lychee is an authentic Thai restaurant smack dab in the middle of the Plateau on Mont-Royal. The dark wood floors, Buddha paintings, glowing fish tank and bamboo blinds create a warm and pleasant atmosphere. There is plenty of room for groups and a row of large booths along one wall for a more intimate meal setting. The appetizers include crispy dumplings, spicy calamari, fish cakes and imperial rolls, but for something more interesting, try the Thai salads. There is a choice of green papaya, or a refreshing cold glass noodle mixture with coriander, shrimp, peanuts and chillies. There are plenty of meal-sized soups to choose from and house specialties with lychees—their signature ingredient. The curries aren't too heavy or creamy, and are served with a perfectly-cooked medley of fresh veggies. All dishes can be made with your choice of vegetables, tofu, pork, chicken, beef, shrimp, duck, scallops or a seafood combo, making the menu pretty accommodating for any kind of appetite. For a comfortable atmosphere and a very pleasing meal out, Lychee will definitely leave you full and happy.

187 Mont-Royal E. (at Hôtel-de-Ville)
514-844-3882
www.restolychee.com
Metro: Mont-Royal
Hours: Tues-Fri 11:30am-2:30pm; Sun-Thurs 5-10pm;
　Fri-Sat 5-10:30pm
Cards: Visa, MC, Interac
Terrace: No
Vegetarian friendly: Yes
Wheelchair access: One step
Price: starters $3.50-$8.95; mains $9.50-$21.95

Lyla

This relative newcomer on the BYO beat is definitely a must for fans of Vietnamese food. Lyla, located on Jean-Talon right next door to Parc metro, serves up delicious, authentic Vietnamese specialties at very affordable prices. With warm yellow-painted walls, kitschy tables and chairs and a sky painted ceiling, the décor is really a toss up between Miami circa 1985 and Nickels. There are outstanding choices to start off with and it's hard to have just one. The mini-Tonkinese soup is excellent, with a rich, full-bodied broth, a sprinkling of fresh herbs and thin noodles. The dumplings are fresh and quickly pan seared, filled with chunks of shrimp and pork and served with a tangy sesame dipping sauce. The Goi Ga salad is a cold, shredded chicken and cabbage combo with a scattering of fresh basil. This is an excellent light and healthy option. The main soup course—Pho—is done right with several different beef options, two chicken choices and a surprising vegetarian alternative. Pork dishes in Vietnamese restaurants are usually a specialty, and Lyla is no exception. The hands-on, DIY grilled pork rice pancakes are a little messy, but absolutely delicious. You roll them yourself adding pork, cucumber, basil, carrots and sprouts. A great dish to share. The staff is helpful and extremely sweet. Lyla is well worth a visit for an outstanding Vietnamese meal.

431 Jean-Talon W. (at Hutchison)
514-272-8332
Metro: Parc, or Place-des-Arts, then bus 80
Hours: Sun-Wed 11am-9pm; Thurs-Sat 11am-10pm
Cards: Visa, MC, Interac
Terrace: No
Vegetarian friendly: Yes
Wheelchair Accesible: Yes
Price: starters $2-$6; mains $6.75-$10.75

Machiavelli

Owned and run by the young, ambitious duo of Ryan Kelly and Raymon Sharma, Machiavelli is an appealing little Italian restaurant in the heart of Point St-Charles. Tastefully decorated with local art and with a great backyard dining area, classic dishes are served with a personal touch. A must-try is the delicious fresh summer bocconcini salad with hand-picked basil from the little herb garden behind the restaurant. The Godfather spaghettini—one of the more popular dishes—is a combination of Italian sausage, sun dried tomatoes, black olives and herbs lightly tossed in olive oil. The flavours are balanced, the pasta al dente, and the results will have you licking your spoon. Their fish and chicken dishes are also equally notable. The highlight of the meal was a blue cheese crème brulée, the saltiness of the blue cheese an excellent savoury balance to the sweetness of this classic dessert. It's impressive to see young people working hard and taking a gamble in a fickle industry. Ryan and Raymon have done their homework and are on the path to success.

2601 Centre, Point-Saint-Charles (at Charlevoix)
514-315-9981
www.machiavelli.ca
Metro: Charlevoix
Hours: Tues-Sun 5pm-9pm
Cards: Major cards, Interac
Terrace: Yes
Vegetarian friendly: Yes
Wheelchair access: One step
Price: starters $5-$12; mains $9-$25

Maison Grecque, La

It often becomes difficult to distinguish between the many Greek BYOs Montreal has to offer. They all look very similar, their menus are practically identical, and most lay claim to fame for their summer terraces. La Maison Grecque is case in point. Inside it has that cavern-like feel with brick archways, several adjoining rooms on various levels, lots of plants and wood paneled walls. Their backyard terrace is homey, surrounded by a Greek blue and white picket fence and covered by leafy trees. The menu offers the usual suspects to start: pikilia, calamari, spanakopita, tzatziki, and taramosalata. The main dishes all include an onion soup, or soup of the day, often lentil. What sets La Maison Grecque apart from the rest is that their food is truly delicious, the prices are more than reasonable, and the service is friendly and personable. Their portions are more than enough, their house salad (although sometimes overdressed), is tasty and the overall quality of the food is superb. The warm garlic bread that arrives at each table is a nice touch. Some of their meat dishes, such as their various brochettes, are drizzled in their house sauce, a honey mustard mixture—a successful combination of Greek spices and sweet mustard. Their lamb shish kebabs are excellent. (Pork has replaced lamb in most Greek restaurants). The selection of desserts is more of the same, but you can't win them all.

450 Duluth E. (at Rivard)
514-842-0969
Metro: Sherbrooke
Hours: Mon-Sun 11am-11pm
Cards: Major cards
Terrace: Yes
Vegetarian friendly: Yes
Wheelchair access: No
Price: starters $2.25-$9.50; mains $10.95-$26.95

Monsieur B

One of the newer BYOs on the Montreal scene, Monsieur B took over the old space in the Plateau that housed the beloved Montée de Lait. With hard shoes to fill, this market cuisine bistro (affiliated with O Thym and Les Infidels) is stepping up to the challenge and serving seasonal dishes that are sure to impress. The restaurant is relatively small, with no more that 40 seats, but feels comfortable and modern, with just enough space to not get that elbow rubbing feeling so many small restaurants can't avoid. The menu is concise, with a soup of the day included in every main course, regardless of entrée. There are seasonal specials like a a finger-licking panna cotta of the summer's first Quebec asparagus resting on a mound of julienned vegetables. Light, refreshing and perfect. Some of the appetizer highlights of Monsieur B are the foie gras with fig compote and brioche toast, delicately seared scallops with butternut squash purée, and a crab cake (packed with the crustacean) with an airy, "mayo-esque" dipping sauce. For mains, the veal filet with mustard sauce was pink and served with polenta and a medley of vegetables, the lamb shank risotto with green peas was melt in-your-mouth delicious, and the baked salmon was crisp on the outside and lightly cooked in the centre with bite-sized cod croquettes and sour cream on the side. To end the meal there is a fine selection of Quebec cheeses and about five sweet desserts—the pistachio brownie being particularly favoured. With meals like this, Monsieur B will thrive.

371 Villeneuve E. (at de Grand-Pré)
514-845-6066
www.monsieurb.ca
Metro: Mont-Royal
Hours: Mon-Sat 5:30-10:30pm, Sun 11:30am-10:30pm
Cards: Visa, MC
Terrace: No
Wheelchair access: A couple of entrance steps
Price: starters $8-$16; mains $20-$30

Mozza

This Italian pasta and pizza spot is located on a busy strip in the heart of Montreal's Gay Village (which becomes a pedestrian mall for the summer months). Although quite small and narrow, the modern design and livelier-than-average music, paired with the subdued lighting and young, hip staff, are proof that BYOs don't have to be stuffy. Chef Jason Kravitz's mantra at Mozza is to create unique and original dishes using only the freshest ingredients. There are two separate blackboard menus— one being the specials for the night and the other, two or three passionate suggestions from the chef. All table d'hôte selections come with a Caesar salad, a choice of starter and a main course. Mozza's pastas on the menu are split up into five different sauce sections, (cream, rose, tomato, olive oil, and cheese) with at least four variations to choose from. They also offer salads, thin crust pizzas and vegetable and meat sautées for those who are cutting their carbs. The flavours at Mozza are simple and the quality of the food stands out. The most surprising part of the Mozza dining experience has to be their awe-inspiring washroom. It definitely wins the top ranking in the city for creativity. Let's just say a disco ball is involved. Check out Mozza for yourself, it's a fun place to dine out with a great atmosphere. Because of its size, reservations are recommended.

1208 St-Catherine E. (at Montcalm)
514-524-0295
Metro: Beaudry
Hours: Mon-Fri 6-10pm; Sat-Sun 5:30-10pm
Cards: Visa, MC
Terrace: Yes
Vegetarian friendly: Yes
Wheelchair access: Yes
Price: starters $3-$12; mains $17-$25

Oggi Ristorante

Oggi is a family-style restaurant run by brothers Renato and Daniele Carpanzano. With their nonna's authentic recipes and true Italian touch, they have managed to create an oasis for Italian home cooking in a West Island mall. Despite the fact that it is a large establishment designed to accommodate parties and groups, with an outdoor dining area for the summer months, the atmosphere is laid-back. When you sit down you are served warm Italian bread with olive oil and balsamic vinegar for dipping. There are plenty of appetizers to choose from. The meatballs are recommended—three moist and fabulous palm-sized polpettes in a rich tomato sauce with just a hint of fresh herbs. This dish undoubtedly has Nonna's Calabrese influence—meatballs like this are treasured family recipes. The pastas offer plenty of meat and seafood choices, and the osso buco with garlic linguine is superb, and generous. Other favourites: veal scaloppini in a white wine sauce with red peppers, capers and black olives, and the grilled chicken with mushrooms, roasted almonds and white wine. Oggi's fare is consistent and whole-heartedly satisfying, with plenty of options for children. The portions are substantial and the service is gracious.

3689 St. John Blvd, DDO (at Blue Heaven)
514-620-0034
www.ristoranteoggi.com
Hours: Sun-Thurs 11am-10pm; Fri-Sat 4-11pm
Cards: Major cards, Interac
Terrace: Yes
Vegetarian friendly: Yes
Wheelchair access: Yes
Price: starters $4-$15; mains $12-$42

O Thym

This stylish and minimalist BYO is located in the Gay Village. A sister restaurant to Les Infidèls, O Thym lives up to expectations. The menu is modern French bistro with an emphasis on lighter dishes with fresh flavours and seafood. Their welcome experimentation with food combinations result in a sophisticated meal in an enjoyable environment. In true bistro style, there are no menus here—the many impressive specials of the day are written on large black chalkboards. Appetizers can include arugula salad with duck magret and shaved parmesan or wonderful seared scallops with mango and chayote salsa. The wait staff are swift and attentive. With plenty of seafood dishes to choose from, O Thym is a welcome departure from the usual French "salmon" alternative to meat. The tuna with curry, honey and grilled coconut and the shrimp with garlic, tomato and pastis are particularily tasty. Another delicious must-have is the crispy pistachio ris-de-veau with apricot sauce. Usually full and bustling, with the sounds of the diners bouncing off the restaurant's tiled floors and high ceilings, O Thym reflects the innovation and good taste of its owners.

1112 de Maisoneuve E. (at Amherst)
514-525-3443
www.othym.com
Metro: Berri UQAM or Beaudry
Hours: Tues-Fri 11:30am-2:00pm; Sun-Thurs 6-10pm;
    Fri-Sat 6-11pm;
    Brunch Sat-Sun 10:30am-3pm
Cards: Major cards
Terrace: No
Vegetarian friendly: Limited
Wheelchair access: Washrooms are downstairs
Price: Lunch $16-$19; Dinner-starters $8-$18; mains $19-$33

Pégase, Le

This quaint restaurant situated in a converted apartment is very popular with the locals of this Gilford-Papineau neighbourhood. And so it should be. The food is terrific and the table d'hôte menu is very reasonable considering what you get. They put a lot of thought into little details here, like the different kinds of bread served with butter, and nice tableware including linen napkins. Indulge in starters such as escargots with carmelised apples and blue cheese sauce, or warm salad of glazed duck with balsamic vinegar. What is especially endearing about Le Pégase is their plate presentation. Interwoven sauces in a variety of ornate and colourful circle and star shapes highlight the food on the plate. It's so retro, it's actually nouveau! The baby scallops in filo pastry with basil and white wine sauce are an artistic creation. If there is something they do extremely well here, it's cooking the meat to a perfect rose. From the succulent duck breast with orange zest to the rack of lamb with two mustard sauce or the ostrich medallion with lingonberry sauce, they just seem to have the talent for getting it spot-on every time. Their Quebec cheese plate and desserts are also well worth the visit, a sumptuous way to end an exceptional meal. Reservations are recommended.

1831 Gilford (at Papineau)
514-522-0487
www.lepegase.ca
Metro: Laurier, then bus 27
Hours: Tues-Sun: 5:30-11pm (Kitchen closes at 9:30pm)
Cards: Major cards
Terrace: Yes
Vegetarian friendly: No
Wheelchair access: A couple of steps
Price: table d'hôte $22-$30; gourmet table d'hôte $33-$41

Piton de la Fournaise, Le

With its blend of European, African, Indian and Chinese culture, Le Piton is a refreshing escape from the usual. It offers the only cuisine in Montreal from Réunion, a French island located in the Indian Ocean east of Madagascar. As with true island living, this space is bright, friendly and unpretentious. The walls are decked out with bamboo panels and plenty of lively artwork. The chairs, tablecloths and napkins are an explosion of vivid colours, and the food is as equally vibrant. The menu includes a page of definitions, but the owners will happily explain and make recommendations. From the light and pleasant watercress soup to the very popular and satisfying shark curry, the portions are generous and the flavours delicately spiced and exotic. Accompanying all main dishes is a trio of zesty salsa-style dipping sauces served in tiny silver cups—eggplant, tomato and lemon—which add a cool fresh contrast to the curries. Other dishes of note are the salad of papaya, mango, carrot, strawberry and crab, or the rabbit breast with coconut milk and cumin. The moist sweet potato cake with a dollop of cream is a perfect (traditional) dessert.

835 Duluth (at St-Hubert)
514-526-3936
www.restolepiton.com
Metro: Mont-Royal or Sherbrooke
Hours: Tues-Sun: 5:30-11pm
Cards: Major cards, Interac
Terrace: No
Vegetarian friendly: No
Wheelchair access: A couple of steps
Price: starters $7.50; mains $24.75-$29.75 (including soup/salad and dessert)

Pizzeria Napolitana

Pizzeria Napolitana has been serving Montrealers authentic Neapolitan pizzas since 1948 and these crispy, thin-crust pies are pretty darn good. There is something very satisfying about a good pizza. It's a fine balance between just the right amount of cheese with a simple medley of ingredients so that the flavours do not overwhelm each other. The perfect base should be thin, crispy and consistent from centre to crust. These good pizzas don't come around too often, but apparently, they've been around for over sixty years in our very own Little Italy. At Napolitana on Dante, you can enjoy great pizzas in a casual setting, with enough tables for groups, a little terrace on the side, and an unusual realistic-looking tree in the middle of the dining room. There are over thirty pizzas to choose from, with just as many pastas and some salads, antipastos and desserts. The Chef and the Amalfitana pizzas are a good choice, as is the spaghetti pescatore and the ravioli biancoverde. The salads are large enough to share. The service is sometimes hurried, as they really pump out those pizzas at an alarming rate, and it's not unusual to see line-ups outside. Naples was the true birthplace of the pizzas we have grown to love and Pizzeria Napolitana is carrying on the tradition.

189 Dante (at De Gaspé)
514-276-8226
www.napoletana.com
Metro: De Castelnau or Jean-Talon
Hours: Mon-Tues 11am-11pm; Wed-Thurs 11am-12am; Fri-Sat
    11am-1am; Sun: 12pm-12am
Cards: Cash only
Vegetarian friendly: Yes
Terrace: Yes
Wheelchair access: 2 steps
Price: $9.50-$17.50

Poisson Rouge, Le

Finally, a restaurant that embraces the bounty of the sea where you can bring your own wine! This bistro for fish lovers also generously offers a few choices for those whose cravings are more carnivorous. With new chef Jeannine Ouellette spicing things up in the kitchen, this modest restaurant is equally appropriate for a blustering winter night as it is for Montreal's infamous summer heat. The décor is clean and bright, and the service is personal, making you feel right at home. The starters span surf with a bit of turf, including escargot, mussels, smoked salmon, cheese, a simple, fresh bocconcini and tomato salad and a prosciutto dish. The mains are more elaborate, with skate wing, sea bass, blackened salmon, Canadian scallops and tuna, but also chicken, duck confit, rack of lamb and sweetbreads. There is the degustation option for $38 that comprises an appetizer, soup or salad, main course, dessert and coffee. This is definitely an extremely good deal considering the freshness of the fish and the size of the portions. Otherwise, you can order an appetizer, soup or salad and main separately. The desserts are always changing and if you get a chance to sample the praline and crepe tart, do yourself a favour. This restaurant is a neighbourhood favourite and fills up fast, so make reservations and get your weekly fish fix.

1201 Rachel E. (at De La Roche)
514-522-4876
www.restaurantlepoissonrouge.ca
Metro: Mont-Royal, then bus 97 (east)
Hours: Tues-Wed 5-9:30pm, Thurs-Sat 5-10pm
Cards: Major cards, Interac
Terrace: No
Vegetarian friendly: Limited to starters
Wheelchair access: No
Price: starters $9-$12; mains $28-$38

Prunelle, La

La Prunelle is a truly pleasurable dining experience. A family-owned restaurant for over ten years, they've recently acquired the talents of chef Sonia Pinel who has put an interesting and innovative spin on classic French cuisine. The space is also unique—the long, rectangular room rolls up its garage-style windows on the front and side of the restaurant to convey the impression you're eating outdoors in the summer. In winter, the windows accentuate the intimacy of La Prunelle. Daily specials appear on a blackboard, along with a tasting menu and spiked sorbet palate cleansers to enhance the experience. Buying local and in season, Pinel combines local Quebec ingredients with influences from around the globe in dishes such as curries, grilled sesame oil hummus and mango and pear chutneys. Mains include rabbit confit with Bleu Benedictin sauce, duck magret with Estafette de Dunham white wine reduction, and a fine lamb filet with herbed crust. The menu is interesting, varied and brings creativity back to the kitchens of Montreal's BYOB dining scene. Many of the desserts are standards such as crème brulée and crème caramel, but the cheese plate, with a selection of three local cheeses for $9, is a savoury steal.

327 Duluth E. (at Drolet)
514-849-8403
Metro: Sherbrooke
Hours: Mon-Sun 5:30-10:30pm
Cards: Major cards
Vegetarian friendly: No
Terrace: No
Wheelchair access: A couple of steps
Price: mains $28-$60

P'tit Plateau, Le

This cozy spot is everything you would want in a corner bistro. It's intimate, warmly decorated and never seems to disappoint with its cuisine from the south of France. In true French style, the small wooden tables are inches away from your fellow diners so if you want some more elbow room, ask to sit at the windows for prime seats which open to the street in summertime. The portions are generous; if you plan to have appetizers bring your appetite. For those who love foie gras, sharing this rich, generous signature dish is recommended. All of the mains come with a choice of soup of the day or salad. A favourite is the red deer—full-flavoured, lean, perfectly medium-rare and served with a beautiful wild berry sauce. The 12-hour lamb shank is melt-in-your-mouth and the cassoulet is superb and often sells out. For those who steer away from meat, the lightly-crusted salmon is an excellent choice. If you happen to have room for a dessert, the crème brulée is delicious. Reservations are highly recommended and if you don't like to feel rushed during your meal, opt for the second seating.

330 Marie-Anne E. (at Drolet)
514-282-6342
Metro: Mont-Royal
Hours: Tues-Sat 5:30-10pm
Cards: MC, Visa
Vegetarian friendly: Limited
Terrace: No
Wheelchair access: No
Price: starters $8-$18; mains $29-$34

Punjab Palace

Jean-Talon between Parc Avenue and L'Acadie has become a street known for it's authentic and affordable Indian cuisine. What was once a Greek neighbourhood has become mainly East Asian with a variety of other ethnic groups and vestiges of the Greek community. Punjab Palace is a spacious, tastefully-decorated family-run labour of love. The menu offers a wide selection of dishes from the tandoor clay oven including the lightly spiced and marinated chicken tikka. It's absolutely delicious when dipped in the accompanying raita. There are also curries, kormas, kadhais (dishes cooked in an Indian version of a wok), some South Indian sambal specialties, and plenty of breads to choose from. All the favourites are here, from the creamy butter chicken to the hot vindaloo. There is a choice of vegetarian dishes like the combination plate thali, channa masala—the classic North Indian mixture of chickpeas, yoghurt and spices. On a hot day, go for the full Indian experience and order a salty lassi to cool off. For dessert, super-sweet gulab jamuns are always a great choice when dunked in a glass of warm, milky chai.

920 Jean-Talon W. (at Stuart)
514-495-4075
Metro: Acadie
Hours: Tues-Thurs 12-10pm; Fri-Sat 12-11pm; Sun12-10pm
Cards: Major cards, Interac
Terrace: No
Vegetarian friendly: Yes
Wheelchair access: No
Price: Inexpensive

Raclette, La

Nestled in among the triplexes of the Plateau, this stylish restaurant gives us a taste of Swiss and European fare. Raclette is a semi-firm cow's milk cheese that is heated and served with small potatoes and eaten with bread, pickled onions and cornichons. It's sinfully good and hard to have just a taste. Luckily for us, it's offered here with the option to order it as an appetizer or main course. The menu includes standard bistro fare—salmon, veal loin, duck breast and a bavette steak—and Swiss touches like cheese fondue (with either pink peppercorns, shallots or tomato), veal à la Zurichoise, cheese crepes with thyme, and the more elaborate main course raclette option. There are two table d'hôte meals which come with either the soup of the day or a glass of vegetable juice. Each table is given little jars of tasty pickled treats that are great to munch on with fresh baguette. In the summer it's a pleasure to sit on the gorgeous front terrace enclosed by a leafy trellis. In the wintertime how could anyone resist hot gooey cheese to warm up? Its refreshing to see Swiss cuisine represented in Montreal's BYO dining scene.

1059 Gilford (at Christophe-Colombe)
514-524-8118
Metro: Laurier, then bus 30 (north)
Hours: Mon-Sun 5:30pm-12am (kitchen closes at 9pm)
Cards: Major cards, Interac
Terrace: Yes
Vegetarian friendly: Yes, if cheese is an option
Wheelchair access: A couple of steps
Parking: No
Price: starters $9; mains $22-$39 (including table d'hôte)

Ristorante Portovino

Portovino is a massive Italian restaurant is just off the Trans-Canada highway in the West Island. Their menu matches their capacity, offering all sorts of Italian specialties across the board. Despite its size—two floors with tall windows, high ceilings with exposed wood beams, and a charming stone fireplace—the décor is sophisticated and warm. Baked in wood fire ovens the pizzas are thin and crispy. There are daily specials and the waiters actually come out with platters to show you the raw seafood, meats, and eventually the desserts, they have to offer. It's a nice touch, and it keeps their friendly staff moving at a very fast pace. Best bets are the Quebec milk-fed veal, Angus beef, osso bucco alla milanese, fresh Atlantic salmon, whole wheat linguini with shrimp, and moules-frites. On Sunday they offer an all-you-can-eat buffet. Portovino's unpretentious, bustling atmosphere with live jazz offers quality Italian food a cut above the standard fare.

1290 Trans-Canada Hwy, Dorval (at Hymus Blvd.)
514-683-8466
Hours: Mon-Wed 11am-10 pm; Thurs-Fri 11am-11pm;
    Sat 4 pm-11pm; Sun 10 am-2 pm, 5pm-10pm
Cards: Major cards, Interac
Terrace: No
Vegetarian friendly: Yes
Wheelchair access: Yes
Parking: Yes
Price: starters: $10-$12; mains $13-$42

Steak Frites St-Paul, Le

Le Steak Frites St-Paul is a Montreal-area chain founded in 1986. This branch opened where Eduardo's used to be on Laurier West. With two stories and ample room for birthdays and parties, this is a great place to go with a bottle of red for a reasonably-priced steak meal. The steaks come in two sizes—the New York Strip, 7oz and 9oz, and the filet mignon, 5oz and 10oz. All steaks are served with a choice of three sauces which are thankfully served on the side. There is also a surf and turf, lamb chops, duck confit and grilled salmon. The fries are the real thing and are replenished without asking. You have a choice of sides like sautéed mushrooms, green beans, or a vegetable brochette. All mains come with a simple Boston lettuce salad dressed with a creamy vinaigrette. The steaks fit the bill but if the place is really busy, it's a good idea to under-order the cooking of your steak (if you like medium, go for med-rare). When the heat's on in the kitchen, your steak could suffer. The original Steak Frites, 12 St-Paul W., in Old Montreal has a lovely terrace. All locations are listed on their Web site.

1014 Laurier W. (at Hutchison)
514 270-1666
www.steakfrites.ca
Metro: Place-des-Arts, then bus 80
Hours: Mon-Thurs 10:30am-10pm; Fri 11am-11pm; Sat 4pm-11pm; Sun 4pm-10pm
Cards: Major cards, Interac
Vegetarian friendly: Barely
Terrace: Not at this location
Wheelchair access: No
Price: starters $5-$13; mains $14-$38

Sushi Mou-shi

Sushi Mou-shi, situated on nondescript Décarie Boulevard, is nothing spectacular to look at, but the fresh, affordable sushi really seals the deal. From edamame beans to shrimp tempura, miso soup to waki-maki, Sushi Mou-shi serves it up fresh and adds their own creative kick to the mix. Although the restaurant is bare-bones simple, they do have a tatami room at the back. To start off, the chicken gyozas are fried and delicious. Crunchy on the outside with an oniony, ground chicken filling—they were absolutely addictive. The tempura is light enough not to overpower the shrimp, the warm edamame beans are sprinkled with sea salt, and the miso soup is flavorful and delicate. The sushi selection allows enough choice for those who like their spicy tuna and Californian rolls to be happy, but also offers exciting house specialties like the waki-maki—a rice paper roll stuffed with spicy salmon, avocado, tempura, carrots and cucumber. There is also a variety of cooked sushi, including chicken and beef rolls, also worth a taste. The teriyaki grilled salmon is perfectly cooked, although the vegetable side is a bit too sweet. What makes this Japanese restaurant truly worth the trip is the bill at the end of the meal. We ate far too much food and gasped at what we paid. There is also an all-you-can-eat menu option for those who want an over-the-top sushi indulgence.

5193 Decarie (at Queen Mary)
514-369-8860
www.sushimoushi.ca
Metro: Snowdon
Hours: Mon-Sun: 5-9:30pm
Cards: Visa, MC
Terrace: No
Vegeterian Friendly: Yes
Wheelchair Access: A couple of entrance steps
Price: starters $2.25-$5.75; sushi $2.75-$5.50; yaki $14-95-$16.95

Terrasse Lafayette

This is a no-frills, neighbourhood eatery that is great for a casual meal out that won't blow the bank. The kitschy 1970s décor is authentic! You expect to see a waitress with a beehive hairdo. Lafayette's great leaf-covered terrace wraps around the building with plenty of plastic tables and chairs *à la* B-B-Q patio style. The menu offers everything—pastas, pizzas, souvlakis, brochettes, subs, burgers and salads. The monster Lafayette burger has a reputation of its own and requires a healthy appetite. For a relaxed meal with friends or family, with a bottle of wine—with no surprises and no disappointments—this is the perfect spot to sit outside and enjoy a summer night. Terrasse Lafayette has the welcoming feeling of a real local hangout where all the patrons live around the corner and everyone knows the menu.

250 Villeneuve W. (at Jeanne-Mance)
514-288-3915
Metro: Place-des-Arts, then bus 80
Hours: Mon-Sun 11am-11pm
Cards: Visa, MC, Interac
Terrace: Yes
Vegetarian friendly: Yes
Wheelchair access: Yes
Price: starters $5.95-$13.95; mains $4.95-$24.95

Toucheh

Toucheh is a Westmount gem that has been serving Italian/Iranian fusion for over ten years. With an open kitchen, quirky wood-panelled walls and homey décor, the table d'hôte menu is written on a plastic wipe board at the back. The owners are always present and are pleased to explain the menu. The dishes, predominantly Italian with a Persian touch, are served with either the soup of the day or a salad. The penne cardinale, in a rosé sauce with chicken and mushrooms, is absolutely indulgent—creamy and garlicky without overwhelming. The chicken scaloppini is served with a delicate lemon sauce and paired with an exceptional garlic and olive oil fettuccine that beautifully complements the dish. The liver is cooked perfectly and also served with fettuccine; the pavé of salmon comes with white beans, rice and a grilled tomato. For dessert there is a rice pudding or a tiramisu, opt for the latter. It's no surprise that Toucheh has a loyal following.

315 Prince-Albert, Westmount (at Somerville)
514-369-6868
Metro: Vendome, or bus 24 on Sherbrooke
Hours: Tues-Sun 5-11pm
Cards: Visa
Terrace: No
Vegetarian friendly: Yes
Wheelchair access: No
Price: mains $17.95-$26.95

Trattoria Il Piatto Pieno

If you're in the mood for the comfort of traditional Italian home cooking, Piatto Pieno is your next dining destination in Little Italy. This bustling and lively environment has been newly-renovated to include a massive backyard patio. The quintessential red-and-white-checkered tablecloths, the solarium (fantastic on blustering winter nights) and the fountain in the patio are signs that you are in an Italian comfort food zone. The food is hearty and the portions are ample. For antipasti you can't go wrong with the grilled vegetables, or Italian sausages with eggplant, and the salads—more than enough for sharing.

Their satisfying pizzas, with a thicker crust, are American-Italian hybrids, and there are plenty of variations to choose from. The pastas, served perfectly al dente, are delicious. For something light and fresh try the Zinghera with shallots, olives, sun-dried tomatoes, artichokes, mushrooms, and peppers in a tomato sauce. The veal and chicken dishes are served with a choice of steamed vegetables or tomato basil pasta (recommended). The classic veal piccata al limone is good bet, or the chicken alla Veneziana made with shallots, garlic, olive oil and lemon. For pleasing retro fare in a high-spirited, boisterous atmosphere this BYO in Little Italy is hard to beat.

177 St. Zotique E. (at De Gaspé)
514-276-1076
www.piattopieno.com
Metro: Beaubien or Jean-Talon
Hours: Tues-Sun 5-9pm (last reservation)
Cards: Major cards, Interac
Vegetarian friendly: Yes
Terrace: Yes, massive
Wheelchair access: Yes
Price: starters $6.95-$14.95; mains $15.95-$20.95

Vivaldi

Located in a strip-mall off Gouin Boulevard, brothers Dave and Steve Droulis have excelled in creating a stylish, tasteful restaurant that offers quality Italian cuisine with service to match. From the long, narrow open kitchen, to the dark wood tables and chairs, the atmosphere of Vivaldi is modern and refined. Their menu offers a wide selection of Italian dishes, from pizzas and pastas, to seafood, beef, veal and chicken. For appetizers, the grilled octopus—slightly charred, brushed with olive oil and served with onions and capers—is exquisite. Also recommended is the eggplant parmesan and their Caesar salad. You could also start by sharing a Marguerita pizza—it's garlic-infused tomato sauce, thin crust and generous cheese—delicious in its simplicity. For mains, the sautéed shrimp in Sambucca with garlic is mouth-watering good. There's a lot to choose from: veal scallopini porcini, chicken cacciatore, grilled Atlantic salmon, peninne all'Caprese (bocconcini and asparagus), and scallops with pesto. For dessert, look no further than the almond cake. It's to die for.

13071 Gouin W., Pierrefonds (at Fredmir)
514-620-9200
www.restovivaldi.com
Metro Henri-Bourassa, then 69 (west)
Hours: Tues-Sun 4:30pm-10:30pm
Cards: Major cards, Interac
Terrace: No
Vegetarian friendly: Yes
Wheelchair access: Yes
Price: starters $2.25-$16.95; mains $12.95-$27.95

Yoyo

Yoyo has been serving classic French cuisine to grateful Montrealers since 1987. Located in a cute little pocket of the Plateau East, it is made up of a series of small connected dining rooms full of characteristic Montreal charm. The menu highlights locally-sourced produce in season, from Quebec lamb to veal bavette, bison ribs and beef tartare. You can't go wrong with the lobster bisque or the minced and crispy pork tart, followed by the lamb shank with red wine jus or the duck magret with maple and blueberry syrup and barley risotto. If you're in the mood to splurge you can start off with their pan-fried foie gras for $23.95, followed by their popular tasting menu for a gastronomic treat. There is good reason why people speak so highly of Yoyo. The food is always of the highest quality, the service flawless, and the portions generous. Restaurants in Montreal don't flourish for twenty years without any merit and this place is a leader. Reservations are recommended.

4720 Marquette (at Gilford)
514-524-4187
www.restoyoyo.com
Metro: Laurier, then bus 27
Hours: Mon-Sun 5:30-10pm
Cards: Major cards, Interac
Terrace: No
Vegetarian friendly: No
Wheelchair access: Yes
Price: starters $6-$18; mains $21-$34

Yuukai Japanese Fusion

This Mile End spot has quickly become a BYO favorite. It's always busy and is great for large groups, including a private room at the back with a large rectangular table that seats up to sixteen people. The décor is subtle. Sliding front windows flood the restaurant with Parc Avenue's eclectic energy in the summer months. The service is delightful and the food is very good. For those who don't want sushi or want to mix it up with a selection of starters, try the beef sashimi, the grilled calamari, the gyoza (beef dumplings) or the Japanese pizza (flat panko crust with raw fish and avocado piled on top). The hot mains include a seafood platter, chicken or beef teriyaki, grilled salmon and the standard tempura options. The sushi is a steal for the price considering the high quality of the fish. There is already a devout Yuukai following among sushi-loving Montrealers. Desserts are limited but the green tea cheesecake always demands several spoons, and the fact that you can bring your own sake and Sapporo, not to mention the SAQ next door for refills, has made it all the more attractive for the hip local crowds.

5658 Parc (at St-Viateur)
514-278-4572
Metro: Place-des-Arts, then bus 80
Hours: Tues-Thurs 5:30-9:30pm; Fri-Sat 5:30-10:30pm
Cards: Visa, MC, Interac
Terrace: No
Vegetarian friendly: Yes
Wheelchair access: No
Price: starters $2.95-$11.95; mains $15.95-$19.95

Zeste de Folie

Although this BYO may be a bit off the beaten path, it is more than worth the detour. Located along a lively strip in Rosemont, Zeste de Folie's tasteful, easy-going atmosphere is no match for its outstanding food. The chef, Yvan, and his partner Sophie, have created sophisticated modern French bistro fare with thoughtful service and attention to detail. With welcome touches such as an amuse-bouche to start, pre-dessert sorbets, and elegant tableware, diners are well taken care of here. The menu is small, but well put together, with nightly specials and a table d'hôte. The menu changes according to the season. The appetizer tartare of the day was an extremely enjoyable mixture of ostrich, bison and duck with nuts, currants and just a hint of chocolate. There was also a refreshing tilapia rillette with lime and the always popular sweet and sour popcorn veal sweetbreads. The main dishes included a bison bavette with gratin, a duck magret with balsamic and red fruit sauce, as well as lamb, veal and seafood dishes. The selection of desserts is tempting, but there is no adenying the pleasure of a homemade lemon tart. Zeste de Folie comes is one of the most exquisite BYO bistros in town, so for head Rosemont and find out for yourself.

3017 Masson (at 7th Ave.)
514-727-0991
zestedefolie.com
Metro: Joliette, then bus 67
Hours: Wed-Sun 5-10:30pm
Cards: Interac
Terrace: No
Vegetarian friendly: No
Wheelchair access: No
Price: starters $8-$14; mains $26-$32

Neighbourhood Index

Cuisine Index

Japanese
Co Ba 30
Sushi Mou-shi 67
Yuukai Japanese Fusion 73

Malaysian
Cash & Cari 26

Mauritian
Delice de l'Île Maurice, Les 33

Moroccan
Couscous Royal, Le 32

North American
Terrasse Lafayette 68

Portuguese
Bitoque 21

Québécois
Colombe, La 31
Entrepont, L' 34
Infidèles, Les 43
Monsieur B 53
Poisson Rouge, Le 60
Prunelle, La 61

Réunionnaise
Piton de la Fournaise, Le 58

Seafood
Poisson Rouge, Le 60

Steaks and burgers
Steak Frites St-Paul, Le 66
Terrace Lafayette 68

Swiss
Raclette, La 64

Thai
Chuch Végé Thaï Express 29
Co Ba 30
Lychee 49

Vegetarian
Chuch Végé Thaï Express 29

Vietnamese
Camelia des Tropiques 24
Feuille de Menthe 36
Fou d'Épices, Le 38
Lotus Bleu 48
Lyla 50